Savannahs

Precious McKenzie

ROURKE
PUBLISHING
www.rourkepublishing.com

www.rourkepublishing.com

PHOTO CREDITS: Title Page: © Vladyslav Morozov; Page Border: © Jason Locke; Page 4, 6: © Jason Register; Page 5, 13: © Nico Smit; Page 7: © BlueOrange Studio; Page 8: © JudiParkinson, © lovleah, © robynmac; Page 9: © AnitaOakley; Page 10: © Deborah Benbrook, © Federico Rizzato; Page 11: © Maxian; Page 12: © Sanai Aksoy, © DavidGarry; Page 14: © gcoles, © Lauzla; Page 15: © Deron Rodehaver; Page 16: © Brooke Whatnall, © clearviewstock; Page 17: © JYLee; Page 18: © Richard Schmon; Page 19: © renelo; Page 20: © brytta; Page 21: © Alex Zanebin

Edited by Kelli L. Hicks

Cover Design by Nicola Stratford   bdpublishing.com
Interior Design by Renee Brady

Library of Congress Cataloging-in-Publication Data

McKenzie, Precious, 1975-
Savannahs / Precious McKenzie.
    p. cm. -- (Eye to eye with endangered habitats)
Includes bibliographical references and index.
ISBN 978-1-61590-317-7 (alk. paper)
ISBN 978-1-61590-556-0 (soft cover)
1. Savannas--Juvenile literature. I. Title.
GB571.M35 2011
578.74'8--dc22
                                        2010009270

Rourke Publishing
Printed in the United States of America, North Mankato, Minnesota
033010
033010LP

www.rourkepublishing.com - rourke@rourkepublishing.com
Post Office Box 643328 Vero Beach, Florida 32964

Table of Contents

What is a Savannah?

Grasslands are on every continent, except Antarctica. Savannahs are grasslands. Savannahs are unique because they are part of the **tropical** grasslands biome.

Savannahs are located in the tropics or subtropics so the temperatures are very warm. The average temperature in a savannah does not drop below 70 degrees Fahrenheit (21 degrees Celsius).

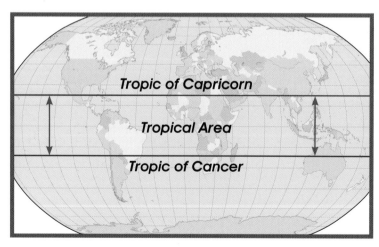

*The tropical area is between the **Tropic of Capricorn** and the **Tropic of Cancer.***

There are two seasons in the savannahs: wet and dry. The dry season has hot winds. The wet season is rainy and there is usually flooding on the low plains.

*Although these two male giraffes look like they →
are acting friendly, they are really fighting!*

Where Can I Find a Savannah?

The Serengeti Plains, in Africa, is the most famous, most photographed, savannah in the world. But, there are other savannahs. There are savannahs in South America and Australia.

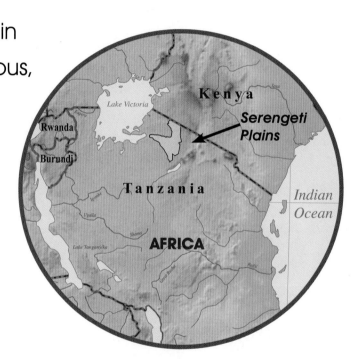

The Serengeti Plains cover almost 5,000 square miles (12,950 square kilometers).

Cheetahs live on the savannah in Serengeti National →
Park, Tanzania. The grasses on the savannah grow
between three and six feet (.91 and 1.52 meters) tall,
providing perfect resting places for cheetahs.

Yummy Grasses and Shrubs

Many different species of animals call savannahs home. Because of the abundance of grasses and **shrubs**, many grazing **herbivores** thrive in savannahs.

Flowers, like the Australian Red Kangaroo Paw plant, grow in the savannah.

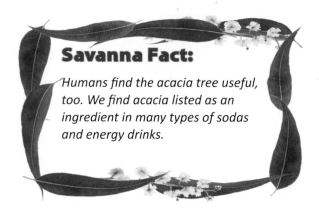

Savanna Fact:

Humans find the acacia tree useful, too. We find acacia listed as an ingredient in many types of sodas and energy drinks.

Acacia trees provide food and shelter → *for many of the savannah's native animals like vultures and zebras.*

The Wild African Savannah

African savannahs have a diverse group of animals. African savannah grazers include elephants, zebras, gazelle, giraffes, antelope, wildebeest, rhinoceroses, and buffalo.

Wildebeest will plunge across rivers to escape dangerous predators.

Naked mole rats and meerkats also make their homes in the warm, tall grasses of the African savannah.

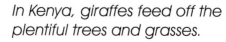

In Kenya, giraffes feed off the plentiful trees and grasses.

Meerkats build their burrows → underground to protect themselves from danger.

Predators!

Grazing animals make delicious meals for the many **predators** of the savannah.

Lions, cheetahs, and hyenas all prey on the African savannahs' diverse wildlife.

Lions usually prey upon weak, young, or solitary animals. Zebras can defend themselves by kicking with their hard hooves and strong hind legs.

Hyenas are not picky eaters. They will feed off of other animals' leftovers.

Do you know how to tell the difference → between a male and female lion? The male lion has a thick mane around his neck.

South American Savannahs

The tropical grasslands, or savannahs, in South America are known as the llanos. The animals that live in the llanos are very different from the African savannah's animals. Anteaters, jaguars, **pumas**, armadillos, and rheas live in the llanos.

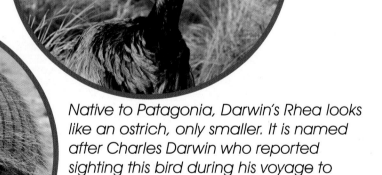

Native to Patagonia, Darwin's Rhea looks like an ostrich, only smaller. It is named after Charles Darwin who reported sighting this bird during his voyage to Patagonia in the nineteenth century.

The Nine-Banded Armadillo is found in Argentina. When frightened, the armadillo will roll itself into a ball.

Pumas, similar to the Florida panthers, prey on the smaller animals that live in the llanos.

Savannahs Down Under

Australia also has savannahs. Australia's savannahs are well known for flat-topped acacia trees.

Kangaroos, wallabies, emus, quolls, and dingoes live in the Australian savannah.

A quoll is a marsupial, which means that a mother quoll carries her baby in a pouch on her stomach.

The yellow footed rock wallaby is a small cousin of the much larger kangaroo. Both animals eat the plants and shrubs in Australia.

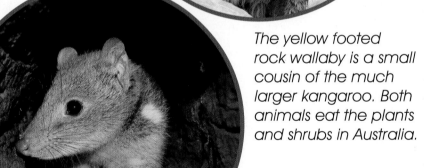

Kangaroos are marsupials, too. →
Mother kangaroos carry their babies, called joeys, in their pouches.

Fire!

Fire is an important part of the savannah's dry season. During the dry season, fire will sweep across the savannah. The fire will burn young shrubs and trees that threaten to **overpopulate** the grassland. The grasses burn, too. But, grass roots survive because they are protected underground. The grass quickly sprouts in the wet season.

The smoke from bush fires can be seen for miles away in the flat savannah. Animals and people must migrate quickly to find safety.

Even though fire makes the landscape look desolate, → the ash from the fire will help the savannah.

Savanna Fact:

Fires leave behind layers of ash and other nutrients that benefit the soil. These nutrients help feed new grasses and plants.

The Threatened Savannah

Humans cause extensive **damage** to savannahs. Ranchers and farmers have altered savannahs for agricultural use. Ranchers allow their cattle and sheep to **overgraze**. Farmers plant rows of crops on what were once open fields of grassland.

Conservationists are working to find ways to balance humans' need for livestock and the savannah's need for plants and grass.

In Africa, the human population is growing and moving from the cities to the savannah. People are building homes, roads, and businesses on the savannah.

Now roads crisscross savannahs, adding a new → dimension to life in the savannah. Animals and people are learning to coexist.

Looking Toward the Future

Scientists are studying new techniques for farming and irrigation that will hopefully reduce the amount of land and water needed to grow crops.

Nations that have savannahs are deciding that savannahs are worth protecting. Some of these nations have established national parks which protect the savannahs by limiting development and prohibiting the poaching of animals.

Perhaps the best hope for preserving savannahs is through **ecotourism**. **Tourists** spend billions of dollars each year to visit savannahs. This money is often reinvested in the national park systems that protect savannahs.

Glossary

damage (DAM-ij): to harm something

ecotourism (ee-koh-TOOR-izhm): a type of traveling that strives to protect and study endangered species and habitats

herbivores (HUR-buh-vorz): animals that eat plants

overgraze (OH-vur-GRAYZ): to allow animals to feed on the grasses too much

overpopulate (OH-vur-pop-yuh-layt): the population is too great to be maintained by natural resources

predators (PRED-uh-turz): animals that hunt other animals for food

puma (POO-muh): another name for a mountain lion or cougar

shrubs (SHRUHBZ): plants that have woody branches near the ground

tourists (TOOR-ists): people who travel for fun

Tropic of Cancer (TROP-ik uhv KAN-sur): an imaginary line around Earth that is 1600 miles (2575 kilometers) north of the equator

Tropic of Capricorn (TROP-ik uhv KAP-ree-KORN): an imaginary line around Earth that is 1600 miles (2575 kilometers) south of the equator

tropical (TROP-uh-kuhl): having to do with the hot, rainy areas of the world near the equator

Index

Websites to Visit

www.nationalzoo.si.edu/Animals/AfricanSavanna/afsavskids.cfm

www.kids.nationalgeographic.com/Animals/CreatureFeature/
    African-elephant

www.mnh.si.edu/mammals/pages/where/africa/savannah.htm

About the Author

Precious McKenzie has spent most of her life in south Florida. She earned degrees in education and English from the University of South Florida. She currently lives in Florida with her husband and three children. They hope to travel to the African savannah someday.

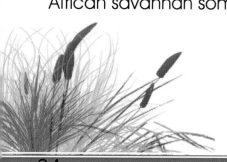